Paradoxical Transformations

by

Holbrook Breckenridge

RoseDog Books
PITTSBURGH, PENNSYLVANIA 15238

RoseDog Books
585 Alpha Drive
Suite 103
Pittsburgh, PA 15238
Visit our website at *www.rosedogbookstore.com*

ISBN: 978-1-6461-0353-9
eISBN: 978-1-6461-0399-7

Dedication

This book has been dedicated in loving memory to my fallen mother, Kalena. Always my rock, paper, and scissors. She was the first to tell me to cut it out. The one to endure the day-in and day-out grind to ensure that I had a sense of self and always first to step up to sacrifice soo much more than a monetary value. Truly, my lost world.

Paradoxical Transformations

Chapter One

In *Celestine Prophesy*, it is mentioned how there once was a sage that came down from heaven. She touched the ground with her right hand and up grew corn, she then touched the ground with her left hand, and up grew potatoes. Upon sitting down, up grew tobacco. What we do not know is if tobacco is a gift like such gifts as corn and potatoes, or if it is the price we pay for such gifts as corn and potatoes.

Riding the highs, lows, and in-betweens in life can naturally bring about states of mania, depression, and neutrality that can make one easily feel feelings of anger, frustration, and indifference. Understanding, nevertheless, that they are still just states of being, it becomes extremely important to acknowledge that ever-so-important cliché of "This too shall pass" for the incorporation of one's versatility in maintaining one's staying power by adjusting one's self accordingly in order to naturally adapt in order to maintain a personal comfort level in whatever environment one may find himself in, in order for one to enhance his odds for staying power if that is his ultimate goal for winning his own personal war within the struggle of his never-ending battle for survival.

When knocked down, it is just as important to pick one's self up by his bootstraps as it is to lend a hand up to the next guy to fall, and it is this admiring adoration and respect that brings out the truest value in the greatest of character. It is easy to kick someone when they are already down, it takes a true hero to opt instead for helping them up. The understanding hero must show restraint, however, in his own understanding that there will always be those who just refuse to get up and with acceptance comes the ability to truly move on to what's next.

The never-ending quest for each of us to find our own way out of our maze and delve into the more surreal and brighter side of life is an achievable ability that we all have; however, it is so often the case that our own personal complications are what more often than not entrap us in a much more complicated maze than we would otherwise have. The underlying silver lining rests in the knowledge that if you can work your way in, upon reversing your actions, you can work your way out. When you are raised with a strong belief in the bible, and over time experience the crucifying inflictions of trying to be perfect in an imperfect world, it becomes easy to denounce religion as a protective mechanism to limit the amount of abuse you receive both internally and externally for the enhancement of a less critical state of being. This is one such example.

Be it as it may, how battles are fought for the sake of competition, and how wars are won by the determining factor of overall competition, there must be a certain level of understanding when making crucial decisions in life that there will often be times whereby battles must be sacrificed for the glory of winning the wars. The same premise holds true when it comes to deal making in how many deals are made with the understanding that they can be renegotiated at a later time. One must always keep in mind that the only thing that is truly final is the point of no return.

When it comes to having children that grow up inheriting certain attributes of their parents, and in some form or fashion, replication inherently occurs, whereby our children become our twins on some level of consciousness, leaving the realization that we are as we have always been, leaves no doubt of how the beginning, middle, and end evolve around the same principle being that what we do is all we have ever known or will ever know when it comes to our own levels of personal understanding and consciousness. Regarding the dead and unconscious, the truth that when you die, you can't be any more dead than the next guy validates the above statement, not only on a practical basis, but on a realistic one as well. There is much grief involved in a story about a dysfunctional separated father-son duo who blame each other for everything because they are exactly alike, including the truth that neither one can tell the other to move out of your mama's house.

As this is now the third book that I have written, there are those who ask how I wrote my books. The truest answer becomes the most basic in explaining; if you can read, then you can write. It only then becomes a matter of articulation, craftsmanship, and production with an underlying understanding that a rolling stone grows no moss. As everyone you meet in life has knowledge that you don't, the key becomes respecting that, as it brings out the best in them as well as you. Often when people are on their way to the top and others see where they are headed, those who are paying attention will tell them not to forget about us little people when you make it big. It is important to note the undeniable truth of how we all rub off on one another and had we not come into contact with influential people, it would have been impossible for us to influence others in neither a positive nor negative fashion for the benefit of becoming the people we are today. The truth undeniably lies in the fact of only after we have been fed are we able to feed.

Referencing tobacco use from the first paragraph of this book in relation to the sage that came down from heaven regarding whether or not the use is to be considered a gift or a price, I have come to notice the majority of those who do smoke have a greater insensitivity to smell than those who don't, most have smaller noses, and in my personal opinion it is not a sin to be born having of a smaller insensitive nose in the overall scheme of things.

Chapter Two

The concept of believing half of what you see and none of what you hear offsets itself by the concept that states the one that speaks learns nothing while the one who listens learns everything. The connecting tissue between both of the above statements lies within the reality that both incorporate some degree of truth. Whether the belief that common sense needs intelligence in order to survive, or having a special knack gives way to great art, the reality that we each encompass a certain level of talent is a world-renowned truth that would prove extremely difficult to disprove. Being this as it may, nurturing such talent for the enhancement of watching it come to fruition may be all in all a highly lucrative process. As with anything else, the importance of giving back, whether coming or going, can pay dividends when it comes to one's balance in staying grounded. Remaining grounded is essential in any transitional state for the benefit of catapulting oneself into the next achievement as well as for the reassurance of one's staying power. At this juncture, you relish in the moment until the decision to apply your talent(s) for what's yet to come, comes.

After one goes through such a cyclical cycle enough times the level of dependability that they experience with themselves and others enhances greatly, and their personal feelings of distrust and fear subsides as their personal independence strengthens. Confidence builds as a result and the underlying belief that there is nothing that is out of reach or unachievable becomes evident. The personal desire to leave any and all negative feelings that coexisted within themselves and others becomes paramount as the acceptance to allow bygones be just that in a new evermore personal quest into the search for truth with an overwhelming feeling of positivity as the primary motivating factor in moving on.

I was once told that in order to catch a unique rabbit, the ability to unique up on him is of utmost importance. The amazing differences in all of us incorporates the underlying tone in how our great uniqueness gives the strongest amount of strength. In looking at our highly versatile world that has, continues to, and forever shall live on long after we are gone. It is this truth that has enabled so much sacrifice for the accomplishment of reaching dizzying heights on such a wide array of levels for the betterment of ourselves and our planet alike. This correlating transition is one that will always exist as it always has and will forever be the common bond within this codependent relationship between mankind and Mother Earth. This bond's common denominator lies in the underlying truth of both man and planet have always and will always naturally transform each other. It is only after the understanding of paradoxical differences that you become aware of the possibility of making paradoxical transitions that ultimately lead you to the acceptance of paradoxical transformations in your life. It is through this unnoticed process that brings about the greatest about face in correcting issues on a personal level that transgress outward into a surrounding level for the enhancement of yourself as well as those around you in the context of progressive growth while moving forward.

Chapter Three

In looking at the upside of making a paradoxical transformation from the bleak and dark side of life to that of a brighter and more positive perspective becomes one that incorporates the transition of difference as beautiful as that of the metamorphic change in a caterpillar into that of a butterfly. As with the chance of a direct correlation between dreaming in one's bed and dreaming throughout a metamorphic state in a cocoon, the difference between an awake state and that of sleep may equally be deceptive throughout a paradoxical transformation. This is best described as not knowing what you have until it's gone, at which point the conversation shifts into the accepting stage of appreciating what it is that you have now acquired. This is highly essential in maintaining one's staying power and understanding what brought you to the point of transformation is of utmost importance to be used in pulling you through.

Like taking the experiences as tools to be used for a modestly prepared journey into the next level of appreciation, it becomes ever so essential to fight the good fight and cut the losses of the bad fights to bring about the more tranquil and easier going you that you remember prior to any transformation that was brought about from any transition that may have really only stemmed from a difference of opinion. The sad truth of how too many battles and wars have been fought over such a trivial subject as that which very easily could have been changed with no more than the inclusion of more information as opposed to such great loss because of a rush to judgment is a truth that one can only learn from as opposed to just pushing it under the rug for it to only re-surface at a later and more unpredictable time.

The largest relational ship error lies within the thinking of how pleasing someone is and much more important than enjoying the company of that of already happy people. When faced with such a predic-ament the importance of self-reflection is important for one's own personal gain. By way of self-criticism, it brings out the best that you have to offer whereas criticizing others brings out their worst. The people you know you can truly trust are those who are happiest when you are happy. Those who aren't can easily be seen as just too self-ab-sorbed and that's okay, seeing how we have all been there before.

The truth that Rome wasn't built in a day dismisses the fact of how people do have the ability to change overnight. As with any transition, the desire to strive is a desire that incorporates desire on any level ex-cept that of reaching a point of no return, referencing that of total ex-tinction in any and all realms whether dead or alive. It is only through this prism that the importance of moving forward for the sake of staying relevant becomes paramount for without this, one is forever trapped in an abyss. The incorporation of this such knowledge brings forth the realization of the importance of appreciation of one's journey in one's personal respect of just how fragile the thread of life truly is. This in turn brings forth the personal gain and wisdom that undoubtedly is needed in the sustainability of maintaining the proper trails life's jour-ney leads you down. Although there is no two of the same rulebooks on parenting, the incorporation of how great minds think alike shall always be there for the taking, for there will always be the common truth of nothing ventured, nothing gained.

While never losing focus on enjoying precious moments along life's twisting road of uncertainty, the importance of finding humor in all that you do and staying forever young in your thoughts and prayers will always find a home in the hopes of your thatch never falling in and you and yours as friends never falling out. Whenever anything met with the best of intentions comes through, the taking of comfort in knowing that you did the best you could will always outshine any and all reservations of negativity that otherwise would have overshadowed such an embarked upon journey.

The only time you are truly able to let your right hand know what your left hand is thinking is if you were born ambidextrous. The ability to totally and completely sync one's body and mind as a God-given right only belongs to those few who are truly gifted to do so. Coming short of such a gift has no bearing, however, in the knowledge that there are those among us that prove how unique we truly are. Embracing such uniqueness becomes one that is commendable in its own right. The ability to marvel at the maverick in ourselves and others is an on-going pastime that often leaves one in a state of awe and amazement, if given the chance.

Chapter Four

Walking the tightrope of feeling positive or negative begins with an appreciation of a profit-and-loss statement for the principled understanding of how all things balance out in the end. It becomes this principle that gives way to a much greater stability that stems from one's security enhanced by one's safety that is encountered upon by one's cooperation with themselves and others alike. It is this premise that gives way to personal choices that include caring about changes that happen through our ability to take chances. These chances are only taken over time by trying as one trust his own personal truth. The understanding of the aforementioned becomes a core ingredient in understanding of how such a paradigmatic principle of how a paradoxical transformation can easily occur.

The fact will always remain that a paradoxical transformation will always be a transformation, nonetheless, regardless of how big or small the change is that occurs, and it is this truth that gives way as to why skittish behavior will always be incorporated in pragmatic behavior for the extra security of limiting inflictions whether internal or external for the benefit of ensuring a greater quality of life for the enhancement of maintaining one's staying power.

As suffering and jubilation coexist to the point whereby one has both laughed until he cries and cries until he laughs again, the ability to take both extremes in stride with the uncanny knowledge that this too shall pass enables a certain resiliency that enables the ability to continue coming back for more. The unrelenting scrutinizing curiosity of "and then what happened" fuels such a thirst for knowledge that the most basic of instincts continue to be driven by way of our natural inquisitive intuition.

Being creatures of habit, we naturally have a distinct tenacity for satisfying any and all of our personal quirks at any given time for our personal satisfaction for the benefit of satisfying the hunger of the beast within. It becomes the importance of learned discipline that enables the civility needed to carry on in a civilized manner for the benefit of different degrees of survival and sustainability. In acknowledging the neutralizing truth that you only digest what you are fed in order to regurgitate it back at a later time, it brings forth once again how the cyclical cycle regenerates itself into never allowing the past to be forever gone from the present and the present from never being too far off from the future as this all becomes relative. It is the juxtaposition of each that gives credence to their importance in both time and space. It is this truth in my opinion that allows such relevance as existence.

As a problem can spring up unexpectedly and easily blindside one that is not expecting it, the follow-through of having ample coping skills to adjust for the benefit of a squash to right the ship, so to speak, prior to experiencing any further damage with the ability of leaving it in the dust from which it first came, can pay dividends in so many more ways that are not solely exclusive to just a monetary value. Through one's experience of surviving the highs, lows, and in-betweens, the development of becoming more and more refined is as great as a slow-cooked homemade meal, and a nice hot shower to follow with a relaxing night's sleep that easily makes way for a brand-new refreshing day.

Chapter Five

J ust as polar as the exchange from day to night and back to day again, the changing of the guard in one's mind can be just as transformative. The cause may be as catastrophic as a worldwide catastrophe, and as small as an electrical impulse, or anything in between. The greatest tool in our toolbox of the mind is that of adaptability, for without that life ceases to exist. The ability, however, being that it can change within itself within a split second's notice, is like that of a double-edged sword in that it can feed and or kill you in an instant. Throughout one's life, this becomes more and more evident whereby the importance of incorporating a strong governing foundation within the context of broadening one's scope through the development of obtaining the widest latitude of education becomes essential, and the versatility associated with it allows for the greatest chance of success in conquering such a paradoxical transformation.

Once such an accomplishment has been achieved the weight of the world is lifted off of one's shoulders, breathing becomes easier as one is in a more relaxed state while anxiety and nervousness fall to the wayside due to a stronger connection with direction between one's body and mind that gives way to clearer thought patterns, which lead to an ability of better understanding that begins a healthier path toward a higher level of enriched wisdom. This path becomes that which is looked forward to being taken as opposed to the prior one being that which has to be taken as the differences become clear.

Fearing negative results upon embarking on this newly desired path greatly subsides as a result of having a newfound positive perspective that has developed upon personally experiencing your own personal transformation, surviving through it, and maintaining the mental capacity to appreciate your battle scars enough to realize that because of them, the initial fear of not surviving on the surface; what appeared to be an impossible feat, in reality, becomes one that is sported about proudly as your own personal badge of honor. The only thing that needs to be addressed at this juncture is the need for keeping one's superiority complex in check for the self-assuredness of refraining from conflicts that can arise from others who may otherwise be forced into dealing with an inferiority complex on their own terms and conditions. It is only after this last piece of the puzzle is correctly put in place that one has all of the tools necessary for the embankment of his now earned, qualified, and anticipated journey, and this becomes the brand-new groundwork in moving on to what's next.

Chapter Six

As with all journeys, the beginning, middle, and end all reside in the cyclical cycle incorporated from the one before, and with the total accepting stage of completion lies yet another higher level of accomplished understanding and wisdom that again prepares one for yet another voyage. These paradoxical transformations occur constantly throughout one's life and quite possibly their afterlife until consequently resting at a point of no return as they very well may be swallowed up within the lifeless belly of an abyss. If one has somewhat of a moral compass, this stage of acceptance can easily come to be with a glorified outlook in that of God very well designed, even this as quite possibly a go-to scenario as he sits back and enjoys watching such a scenario unfold. This is just one example of how broad of a scope in one's thought process can be reached after surviving such a survival trip of growing through such a transformational ordeal in passing from one side to the next in a paradoxical transformation.

After going through such an ordeal and looking back, it becomes easy to ask what was it all for when in reality the healthier perspective is the one of appreciation for having such an opportunity to experience such an experience that otherwise would never have surfaced let alone reach the capacity of being able to wrap one's head around it for such a personal asset as opposed to a detriment as how something will always remain better than nothing, and for having the ability to right one's own ship is equivalent to finding a needle in the haystack from within, ripping it out, and showing it off for all the world to see. The beauty of it all lies within the silver lining of gaining something from which something was ventured on and by way of will and pure determination accompanied by great timing and some luck becomes that which is successfully achieved.

The paradoxical transformational understanding of how such transformations occur begins with acknowledging certain repetitive identifiers that form certain similar patterns that repeat holistically over time as they develop similar repetitive cyclical cycles that upon further explorations give way to well-versed non-biased conclusions, which give fundamental evidence in order to base one's opinion on. As with any opinion, the ability to become open for debate through discussion for the enhancement of one's personal growth becomes enhanced through such dynamics involved, which in turn quite possibly may lead to that of society's growth as a whole. This shows how the impact of one idea can change the dynamic landscape from which all who are involved live, and it is within the context of such a paradigm that easily shows how some of the most ordinary of people achieve the most extraordinary feats in becoming some of life's greatest game changers. Although there is a certain amount of truth in knowing how everyone is needed, yet no one is necessary, it does not change the fact of how no one is insignificant.

Chapter Seven

The indifferent thinking of how life is much to do about nothing becomes easily offset by understanding how idle hands become makers in a devil's workshop. The importance of staying motivated for the enhancement of staying focused to ensure one's staying power and quality of life becomes that of a self-fulfilling health-conscious decision. In respecting the personal individuality of each person's decision-making process, it becomes apparent how limitations do exist within us all, which only validates how a hero's acceptance of loss for the saving of the greater good correlates with how battles are sometimes sacrificed for winning the overall competition of a war. It is this understanding that brings about a fundamental understanding in surviving a paradoxical transformation.

Having the wherewithal to psychologically shock one's state of mind to transgress forward through shocking it back at a later time as a survival tool used for bypassing a catastrophic experience is no different than having to reboot anything for the enhancing purpose of getting rid of a glitch. As in battle, even having the ability to retreat can become a strategic ability, nonetheless, seeing how perseverance will always be based in the epitome of drive as we are all driven by that of basic instinct that will always be controlled by that of electrical impulse.

In adjusting for human error, the essential key becomes that of remaining vigilant with regards to personal glitches that can easily short circuit one's personal mainframe when maintaining such an ongoing work as one's body-mind connection. If everything appears to be great, the realization in how there is nothing greater than experiencing the game of life for nothing more than the congratulating feeling of enjoying the completed satisfaction of relishing in the many toasts of cheers becomes priceless.

The change from being inconsistent to that of consistency becomes a crucial aspect within transition for succeeding in a positive paradoxical transformation, for without it such a transformation will never occur. Witnessing such a paradoxical transformation, however, will forever leave one with a completed sense of accomplishment that will remain closely embraced by their heart and mind for all the days of their life in conjunction with the carefree feeling of not being concerned with such trivial things like a cigarette or cigars, especially after having come to understanding that a torch is made by way of wrapping a newly cut branch with cloth, dipping it in kerosene, and lighting it on fire in order to light a darkened path for the added benefit of moving forward.

Much truth lies with Darwin's "Survival of the Fittest " theory with respect to natural selection when encompassing both body and mind strength with regards to that of having a strong connection to enable the best direction to embark on regarding any road traveled in life whether twisting, forked, or straight. It becomes this, and this alone, that brings forth the much needed versatility for surviving such paradoxical transformations associated with the uncertain trials and errors that may or may not arise in such a unique and unpredictable world, and it is this undying correlation between our planet and ourselves that creates the ability to coexist for whatever amount of time we have together.

This exploratory reality coupled with one's respect in personal space allows for a sense of safety, security, stability, and cooperation when it comes to living one's life using boundaries in order to always remain reasonable to one's self and others for one's own reassurance for maintaining a reasonable quality of life for as long as one shall live. Caring about one's choices in taking chances for the creation of change begins with taking the time to try and trust one's own personal truth for the enhancement of one's safety in order to feel secure and stable for one's personal ongoing quest for cooperation with themselves and others. It is this that becomes one's greatest strength in negotiating that of a better life.

Chapter Eight

Transitioning into the next transition is a transition in itself being that such things as time and space are such God-given entities that allow such a transition to take place in the first place. The same principle holds true with paradoxical transformations in that both encompass the same ability by way of both being mutually inclusive in that of a cyclical cycle. The only true considerations that come into play pertaining to one's freedom of ability is that of choosing to enjoy the ride, go along for the ride, screw up the ride, or get off of the ride altogether. This becomes the most personal decision that one can make, continues to make, or has already made, and whatever that is, the knowledge that acceptance is the final stage of anything before moving on to what's next, what becomes the question in what it is that one is to do with what's next. The propulsion forward is driven forward by the same personal inquisitiveness that we all embody at our core of curiosity. It is only in the satisfying acceptance of quenching our curiosity's thirst that on many levels we become content until that of our next intriguing moment comes about.

Regarding both a desire for suffering and intrigue, the reality of having seen nothing until one's head is washed by that of a black widow spider woman in effect and experience that many would naturally prefer not to experience being that such an experience borderlines that of being scalpcd. In taking roads that are often less traveled, whereby many find much more entertaining than the redundant humdrum of the "same old same old," often the correlation between experience and shock parallel one another on every level. Finding the moderate balance at whichever level one is on is what in effect becomes a crucial piece to the puzzle for ensuring one's chance of paradoxically transforming any extreme circumstance into a much more modest state of balance. The reality alone of how transformations do occur whether in life or death leads one to a final conclusion being that one truly does not know in reality who completely and totally truly dies if anyone at all. It is my personal belief that God owns everyone's failures and victories but not everyone's responsibilities, and throughout any paradoxical transformation it becomes the responsibility of each individual to meet one's basic needs prior to allowing any wants to come into play. The resting acknowledgment will always lie in the unwavering truth that unlike God, heroes will always be created and never self-made. The hardest part of dealing with success is accepting the realization, after acquiring gained knowledge, that there will always be those who just don't want to hear about it due to the reality of how it is often so much easier to just stay content. When looking at all life that continues to exist, it becomes paramount to always keep in mind of how the nurturing hand of nature and the nature of the nurturing hand is great.

Life mimics that of a piece of hologram art in how there are those who simply see life and those that simply live life. The connection lies in the experience of life itself. A good rule of thumb in staying within the boundaries of staying grounded and humble resides in the tale that states: "In the land of the blind, the one who could see would not be king as most would suspect, for he would be killed instead because of doubt." It appears to me that there will always be those who have preconceived notions or biases and those who don't. Then there are those who have become too numb to care because of too many failed attempts at caring. The silver lining resides in finding brilliance within such failures, and milking it for all that it's worth.

Contributions Page

Best regards to the vast array of individuals that have made this book possible. Taking consideration and gratitude into account, the contributions are entirely too great for anyone to repay upon looking at the experience that I have been so blessed to receive. My only hope is for the reader to remain youthful within the aspects of enjoying one's life. At my core I feel that we are all surviving under the same sky and be it as it may, that is nevertheless common ground. The common thread that connects life and death is the constant of time and the understanding that in life we have two choices: to live in peace or rest in peace. Either way, peace prevails.